Black
Achievement
IN SCIENCE

Technology

Mason Crest

Black
Achievement
IN SCIENCE

Biology

Chemistry

Computer Science

Engineering

Environmental Science

Inventors

Medicine

Physics

Space

Technology

Black
Achievement
IN SCIENCE

Technology

By MARI RICH
**Foreword by Malinda Gilmore and Mel Poulson,
National Organization for the Advancement of
Black Chemists and Chemical Engineers**

Mason Crest
450 Parkway Drive, Suite D
Broomall, PA 19008
www.masoncrest.com

Series ISBN: 978-1-4222-3554-6
Hardback ISBN: 978-1-4222-3564-5
EBook ISBN: 978-1-4222-8331-8

First printing
1 3 5 7 9 8 6 4 2

Produced by Shoreline Publishing Group LLC
Santa Barbara, California
Editorial Director: James Buckley Jr.
Designer: Patty Kelley
Production: Sandy Gordon
www.shorelinepublishing.com
Cover photograph by MBI/Dreamstime.

Library of Congress Cataloging-in-Publication Data

Names: Rich, Mari, author.
Title: Technology / by Mari Rich ; foreword by Malinda Gilmore and Mel Poulson, National Organization for the Advancement of Black Chemists and Chemical Engineers.
Description: Broomall, PA : Mason Crest, [2017] | Series: Black achievement in science | Includes bibliographical references and index.
Identifiers: LCCN 2016002450| ISBN 9781422235645 (hardback) | ISBN 9781422235546 (series) | ISBN 9781422283318 (ebook)
Subjects: LCSH: African American engineers--Biography--Juvenile literature. | African American scientists--Biography—Juvenile literature. | Technology--History--Juvenile literature.
Classification: LCC TA157 .R4956 2017 | DDC 620.00922--dc23
LC record available at http://lccn.loc.gov/2016002450

Contents

Key Icons to Look for

 Words to Understand: These words with their easy-to-understand definitions will increase the reader's understanding of the text, while building vocabulary skills.

 Research Projects: Readers are pointed toward areas of further inquiry connected to each chapter. Suggestions are provided for projects that encourage deeper research and analysis.

 Text-Dependent Questions: These questions send the reader back to the text for more careful attention to the evidence presented here.

 Series Glossary of Key Terms: This back-of-the-book glossary contains terminology used throughout this series. Words found here increase the reader's ability to read and comprehend higher-level books and articles in this field.

 Educational Videos: Readers can view videos by scanning our QR codes, providing them with additional educational content to supplement the text. Examples include news coverage, moments in history, speeches, iconic moments, and much more!

cience, Technology, Engineering and Mathematics (STEM) are vital to our future, the future of our country, the future of our regions, and the future of our children. STEM is everywhere and it shapes our everyday experiences. Science and technology have become the leading foundation of global development. Both subjects continue to improve the quality of life as new findings, inventions, and creations emerge from the basis of science. A career in a STEM discipline is a fantastic choice and one that should be explored by many.

In today's society, STEM is becoming more diverse and even internationalized. However, the shortage of African Americans and other minorities, including women, still exists. This series—*Black Achievement in Science*—reveals the numerous career choices and pathways that great African-American scientists, technologists,

By Malinda Gilmore, NOBCChE Executive Board Chair and
Mel Poulson, NOBCChE Executive Board Vice-Chair

engineers, and mathematicians have pursued to become successful in a STEM discipline. The purpose of this series of books is to inspire, motivate, encourage, and educate people about the numerous career choices and pathways in STEM. We applaud the authors for sharing the experiences of our forefathers and foremothers and ultimately increasing the number of people of color in STEM and, more specifically, increasing the number of African Americans to pursue careers in STEM.

The personal experiences and accomplishments shared within are truly inspiring and gratifying. It is our hope that by reading about the lives and careers of these great scientists, technologists, engineers, and mathematicians, the reader might become inspired and totally committed to pursue a career in a STEM discipline and say to themselves, "If they were able to do it, then I am definitely able to do it, and this, too, can be me." Hopefully, the reader will realize that these great accomplishments didn't come easily. It was because of hard work, perseverance, and determination that these chosen individuals were so successful.

As Executive Board Members of The National Organization for the Professional Advancement of Black Chemists and Chemical Engineers (NOBCChE) we are excited about this series. For more than 40 years, NOBCChE has promoted the STEM fields and its mission is to build an eminent cadre of people of color in STEM. Our mission is in line with the overall purpose of this series and we are indeed committed to inspiring our youth to explore and contribute to our country's future in science, technology, engineering, and mathematics.

We encourage all readers to enjoy the series in its entirety and identify with a personal story that resonates well with you. Learn more about that person and their career pathway, and you can be just like them.

Anyone living in about 3500 BCE, after the Bronze Age had arrived in some parts of the world, might have witnessed what was then the height of technology: the first wheel. During the Industrial Age, which began in the mid-18th century, cutting-edge technologies included the steam engine and the machine-powered textile loom. The phrase "high-tech" obviously has different meanings depending on the historical period in question.

The basic definition of technology, however, remains the same: anything invented by humans—tools, materials, or processes—that makes life easier or solves problems. We're now said to be in the midst of the Information Age, sometimes called the Computer Age or the Digital Age. Many modern historians assert that the Information Age had its genesis back in the late 1940s, when mathematician and engineer Claude E. Shannon published a revolutionary paper proposing that all

We are living in a time when the world is at our fingertips, whether on computers . . .

. . . or on smartphones. Thousands of jobs are being created and new careers are starting every day in the enormously wide-ranging fields of technology.

information could be quantitatively encoded as a series of ones and zeroes. By the 1970s, when the US government developed the Internet, and the 1980s, when personal computers became widely available, it was undeniable that the world had entered into an entirely new age.

New technologies have changed the way we work and play, and African Americans, while still underrepresented in the tech fields, have made several important contributions.

In the final chapter, read more about why diversity in the tech arena is so important and find out about possible paths to a high-tech career. ●

Words to Understand

integrated circuit
a set of electronic circuits on one small plate (or chip) of semiconductor material, normally made of silicon

Silicon Valley
a nickname for the area south of San Francisco with numerous high-tech companies, so called because silicon is the most common semiconductor material used to create computer chips

transistor
a device that regulates current or voltage flow and acts as a gate for electronic signals

Chapter 1

Frank Greene

Born:
1938

Died:
2009

Nationality:
American

Achievements:
Inventor and electronics engineer whose work was key to building Silicon Valley powerhouses

While Silicon Valley is still not known as a showcase of racial diversity, Frank Greene is widely credited for making the initial crack in its color barrier back in the 1960s. As an employee at Fairchild Semiconductor, a company that played a key role in the history of **Silicon Valley**, Greene designed **integrated circuits** that became key components of the Illiac IV, then the most powerful computer in the world. He also went on to found two technology companies of his own—a feat nearly unheard of for a black man in that era. Later in life he launched New Vista, a high-tech venture firm that funded many minority-owned start-ups. "Success in life is not about 'me' but about what you can do to help others," he asserted to one interviewer.

Greene was born on October 19, 1938, in Washington, D.C., to Frank S. Greene, Sr. and

the former Irma Olivia Swygert. He grew up in a highly segregated section of St. Louis, Missouri, a place, he once said, where "making it through life was a civil-rights activity in itself." A bright and highly motivated student, Greene attended St. Louis's Washington University, joining only the second class in school history to accept students of color. While there, he was active in the burgeoning civil rights movement and participated in several sit-ins—a form of nonviolent protest in which demonstrators occupy a racially segregated restaurant or bus station and refuse to leave until they are either served or the police come to arrest them.

Greene lived through a time when sit-ins like this one in 1968 were part of a growing Civil Rights Movement.

Once, he and his fellow protestors entered a local pizza parlor, expecting to be denied service. They were thus shocked when a waitress approached them to take their order. So certain were they that they would meet with failure that they hadn't thought to bring any money. "From that day, I've always said, 'You have to be prepared for opportunity when

African Americans have long played a part in the success of the military.

it arrives,'" he explained during an oral history interview archived at the HistoryMakers website. "You've got to be prepared for success."

Greene earned a bachelor's degree in electrical engineering in 1961 and then entered Purdue University, where he earned his master's degree the following year. He then took a break from academia, joining the US Air Force and serving as an electronics engineer for four years. As part of his duties, he reportedly helped develop high-performance computers for the National Security Agency.

Upon being discharged, Greene took a job with Fairchild Semiconductor, a company that had gotten its start a decade earlier, when Nobel Prize-winning physicist William Shockley, co-inventor of the **transistor**, launched an eponymous venture, Shockley Semiconductor. Within a year,

however, eight younger scientists (the "Traitorous Eight," as they were widely known) defected and used their own money to develop a method of mass-producing silicon transistors relatively cheaply and efficiently. With the help of a $1.5 million investment from Fairchild Camera and Instrument Corporation, on October 1, 1957, their new company, Fairchild Semiconductor, was founded. ("The Eight" shipped their first order—100 transistors that they had sold to IBM for $150 each—in an old carton from the supermarket.)

By the time Greene joined the enterprise, Fairchild was well on its way to revolutionizing the computer industry, and he helped greatly in that mission; Greene's name is on the patent for the integrated circuit that made the company an undisputed industry leader in the late 1960s. (Integrated circuits could be made much, much smaller than separate circuits made from several separate electronic components. That was a key breakthrough in the ongoing drive to make computer parts smaller.)

Greene, who in 1970 earned a Ph.D. from Santa Clara University, later

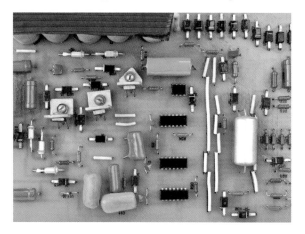

Greene was part of the team that created the first integrated circuits, which have come a long way since.

opened Technology Development Corporation, a computer software and technical services company that had more than 300 employees and annual revenues of more than $30 million by 1985, when it went public. That year, he founded a second firm, Zero One Systems, which was later acquired by Sterling Software.

Greene entered a new phase of life in 1993, when he became a founding general partner of New Vista Capital, helping young entrepreneurs, many of them minority members or women, launch their own tech companies.

As part of his mission to attract greater numbers of students to STEM topics, Greene also taught at Stanford, Howard, Santa Clara, Northwestern, and Washington universities, and he was the founding president of GO-Positive, an organization that offered leadership programs to promising high school and college students. (He was the inspiration behind another nonprofit initiative, the Dr. Frank S. Greene Scholars Program, which encourages California students to pursue STEM studies.)

Greene, who died on December 26, 2009, was inducted into the Silicon Valley Hall of Fame in 2001 for his groundbreaking work and devotion to his field. ●

Words to Understand

entrepreneur
a person in business who starts companies or launches new products

transmitter
a device that sends or passes along an electronic signal

Chapter 2

Gerald A. Lawson

Born:
1940

Died:
2011

Nationality:
American

Achievements:
Inventor and pioneer of early video game technology

The earliest home computer games like Pong were built directly into the hardware, meaning that players could not switch to different games once they had purchased a given system. Gerald A. Lawson, who worked as an engineer at Fairchild Semiconductor, developed the innovative Fairchild Channel F game console, the first ever to use interchangeable game cartridges, greatly expanding the possibilities for home gamers and changing the course of the entire industry.

"Before disc-based systems like PlayStation, Xbox and Wii transformed the video game industry, before techno-diversions like Grand Theft Auto and Madden NFL and even before Pac-Man and Donkey Kong became the obsession of millions of electronic gamers, it was Lawson who first made it possible to play a variety of video games at

home," a tribute published in *The New York Times* acknowledged after he died in 2011.

Lawson, who was generally known by his nickname, Jerry, was born on December 1, 1940, in New York City, and he and his brother, Michael, were raised in a housing project in the borough of Queens. His paternal grandfather had been trained as a physicist, but as an African American, he found it difficult to find related work and instead took a job at the post office. Lawson's father worked as a longshoreman but was a well-read man who was deeply interested in science. He purchased chemistry sets and electronics kits for his son and once gave him an Irish mail cart, a type of scooter operated with a crank, which even later in life Lawson remembered with particular fondness.

Lawson's mother was equally focused on her son's development, and she felt little compunction about giving a false address to a school board or engaging in other subterfuge if it meant that he could attend academically rigorous schools in better neighborhoods. At one school, where he was one of the very few children of color, she was elected president of the PTA.

Larson got his start tinkering with old radio parts.

In addition to his parents, Lawson cited his first-grade teacher,

Ms. Guble, as an important supporter. "[She put] a picture of George Washington Carver on the wall next to my desk. And she said, 'This could be you,'" he recalled to an interviewer for VintageComputing.com. "I can still remember that picture, still remember where it was. . . . This kind of influence is what led me to feel, 'I want to be a scientist. I want to be something.'"

As a teen, Lawson spent almost every Saturday hanging around a local electronics store called Lafayette Radio. Using his small allowance, combined with the money he earned fixing his neighbors' television sets, he gradually purchased enough parts to build his own **transmitter** from scratch and launched an amateur radio station in his bedroom, with the antenna hanging out of the window.

After attending City College and Queens College, both part of the public City University of New York (CUNY) system, Lawson took a series of engineering jobs at such companies as ITT, Grumman, and PRD Electronics. In the 1970s he moved from New York to the West Coast, attracted by the burgeoning computer scene in the San Francisco Bay Area. There he became one of only two black members (the other being **entrepreneur** and inventor Ron Jones) in the now-iconic Homebrew Computer Club, whose best-known participants included Steve Jobs and Steve Wozniak.

In California, Lawson found work with Kaiser, a company specializing in making electronic displays for fighter jets and other military applications. He soon made the move to Fairchild, a full-service semiconductor company

that had produced a microprocessor called the F8. When officials at the company discovered that Lawson had built a coin-operated arcade game called Demolition Derby in his garage, using the F8, they asked him to head their fledgling home video game console project.

The Fairchild Channel F hit store shelves in 1976 and carried a retail price of $169.95. Lawson has told interviewers that he made the mistake of going into the office the day after Christmas that year; with only one other person there, he ended up fielding dozens of calls from consumers, who asked how to replace the batteries on the unit (it had none), what to do if their pet urinated on it, and other such questions.

More than 20 cartridges (which the company marketed as "videocarts") were ultimately released, each selling for $19.95. The variety, while an enormous novelty in the 1970s, might seem exceptionally basic to today's gamers; titles included Alien Invasion, Backgammon, Memory Match, Bowling, Checkers, and Hangman.

While the Channel F console never attained the success of later models from Sega, Atari, or Nintendo, the console made possible an entirely new chapter in video gaming history, and Lawson is widely hailed as a pioneer.

Upon leaving Fairchild in 1980, Lawson launched his own company, Videosoft, intending to create games for the Atari 2600, which by then had made the Channel F virtually obsolete. Videosoft ultimately developed only one cartridge, Color Bar Generator, a tech tool rather than a game,

designed to cal-
ibrate the color
on a television
set and adjust the
vertical and hor-
izontal picture.

In later years
Lawson suffered
from ill health;
even as his phys-

The Fairchild Channel F home-gaming device that Larson invented was a game-changer.

ical condition declined, however, he still enjoyed attending gaming conventions and industry expos, where he was sometimes swamped by gamers who possessed a sense of history and who appreciated his contributions to the field.

Lawson died on April 11, 2011, somewhat disillusioned by the state of modern gaming. "I don't play video games that often; I really don't," he said a few years before he died. "First of all, most of the games that are out now—I'm ap-palled by them. They're all scenario games concerned with shooting somebody and killing somebody. To me, a game should be something like a skill you should develop—if you play this game, you walk away with something of value. That's what a game is to me." ●

Jerry Lawson:
Video game inventor

Words to Understand

corporate board
a body elected to govern a corporation on behalf of shareholders

startup
a newly established business

dichotomy
a division into or distinction between two groups that differ greatly

Chapter 3

John W. Thompson

Born:
1949

Nationality:
American

Achievements:
Technology executive who became chairman of the board of Microsoft

T he nonprofit Alliance for Board Diversity is dedicated to the idea that **corporate boards** work best when they include qualified women and minorities with diverse talents, backgrounds, and perspectives. A recent report by the group found, however, that blacks constitute only 7.4 percent of board members at American companies. One high-profile exception to that dismal news is John W. Thompson, who joined Microsoft's board in 2012, after holding leadership positions at IBM and Symantec, and became the chairman of the software giant in 2014. Concurrently, he heads a relatively new tech company, Virtual Instruments. "I never had any expectations of being anything more than a salesman at IBM and lo and behold, here I sit as the chairman of Microsoft and the CEO of a **startup**," he once marveled to an

interviewer. "That's about as big a **dichotomy** as you could possibly imagine."

John Wendell Thompson was born on April 24, 1949, in Fort Dix, New Jersey. The family later moved to West Palm Beach, Florida. He credits his father, a postal worker, and mother, a teacher, with instilling in him a strong work ethic and good values. Still, he admits, he was far from a model student.

During his senior year at Florida A&M University, a fraternity brother who worked in the office of career services suggested he had the personality to work in sales for a large company like IBM. After he earned his bachelor's degree in business administration in 1971, Thompson joined IBM's sales force. With his outgoing personality and unbeatable sales record, he earned regular promotions. By 1993 Thompson, who had earned a master's degree in management science at MIT in the interim, was the general manager of IBM Americas, a division of the company worth $37 billion, with 30,000 employees under his charge.

In 1999 Symantec, a large but floundering tech company, approached Thompson about taking over for their departing CEO. He left IMB to take the job, and during his decade as CEO, Symantec's revenues grew from $600 million to about $6 billion.

When Thompson retired from Symantec in 2009, he had no plans ever to helm a company again. He thought he might begin investing in startups and serving as an advisor to businesses. Among the first companies to attract his attention was Virtual Instruments, which developed products that monitored the performance of applications in virtual and cloud computing environments. He stepped in as CEO in 2010, intending to stay a few months. Many of the investors he approached, however, agreed to fund the enterprise only if he stayed on as its head.

Now CEO of a young company needing a lot of guidance—and retirement at that point just a distant dream—he agreed in 2012 to sit on the board of Microsoft. Two years later he became the chairmain. In that capacity, he led the search for a new chief executive to replace the departing Steve Ballmer. (Ultimately, Satya Nadella, an Indian-American tech executive, was chosen, making Microsoft one of the few major American companies to have both a minority CEO and a minority board chair.)

Undeniably one of the most iconic and respected African-American figures now working in the tech industry, Thompson has said: "I'm not here to create an image of myself as some black messiah in Silicon Valley. But…they will never say I failed because I was distracted. And they'll never be able to say I succeeded because I was black." ●

John W. Thompson:
Microsoft board chairman

Words to Understand

microchip
a group of small electronic circuits that work together on a very small piece of hard material, such as silicon

video compression
the process of encoding digital video so that it takes up less storage space and transmission bandwidth

Marc Hannah

Born:
1956

Nationality:
American

Achievements:
Creator of early digital special effects and computer graphics

teven Spielberg could not have made the blockbuster film *Jurassic Park*, with its eerily realistic dinosaurs, without the help of Marc Hannah. The villain in the futuristic hit *Terminator 2* might have been somewhat less terrifying without Hannah's input as well. Many movies made over the last few decades, in fact, owe their success in some part to the technology developed by Hannah, an electrical engineer and the co-founder of Silicon Graphics Incorporated (SGI), a company widely celebrated for its innovations in the field of computer graphics.

Hannah was born on October 13, 1956, in Chicago, Illinois. His father, Huber, was an accountant, and his mother, Edith, was a teacher. Both were devoted members of Chicago's Trinity United Church of Christ.

He has recalled being one of the few chil-

dren of color at Fort Dearborn Elementary School, but has described his upbringing as unexceptional in most other ways. His was a typical middle-class family, with parents who stressed the importance of faith and the value of getting a good education to Hannah and his four siblings.

As a youngster, Hannah loved *Star Trek* and other science fiction shows, as well as police dramas and westerns. He has also cited Motown music and Chicago's Museum of Science and Industry as the cultural touchstones of his youth.

As a teen, Hannah initially attended the University of Chicago Laboratory School—a prestigious, but costly choice his parents had made after much deliberation. Following his freshman year, however, he transferred to the Kenwood Academy High School, a new tuition-free school that had just been established on the city's South Side that was attracting a bright and diverse student body. During his senior year he took a computer class that sparked his interest in technology. (He has clarified to interviewers that in the early 1970s, computers were still massive machines owned only by universities, major business-

When Hannah began work in computers, they were operated with these punch cards.

es, and government agencies.) "In the case of the course I had in high school, the computer wasn't at the school," he explained during an oral history interview posted on the HistoryMakers website. "It was somewhere at the end of a phone line. And what we had at the school was a keypunch machine so you could punch cards that would [comprise] the program [that was fed] into the computer."

Hannah, who had long enjoyed tinkering with home electronics alongside one of his older brothers, vacillated between wanting to study physics or electrical engineering in college. He ultimately chose the latter, and in 1977, funded by a scholarship from Bell Labs, he earned his B.S. degree from the Illinois Institute of Technology (IIT), an inner-city school with only bare-bones computer and lab facilities. He then entered Stanford University, where he earned both his master's and doctoral degrees (in 1978 and 1985, respectively.)

"I felt IIT prepared me very well [academically] for Stanford," he recalled in his oral history interview. "[But] as far as computing equipment, there was a building down at the end of the campus that had these mainframes in a room, and you would sit and punch cards and submit it back over a counter. And then you'd get the printout back. So that was the level of technology that IIT was dealing with. And you get to Stanford and there's computer terminals everywhere and they had mainframes [and] access to computers that were donated for research purposes. And there was just computing everywhere you looked...a wealth of facilities."

While at Stanford, Hannah studied under Jim Clark, a professor who was working on a project called the Geometry Engine, a **microchip** that could render sophisticated 3D images based on geometric models. (Previously that level of work had to be done on massive mainframe computers.) Seeking to commercialize his research, Clark amassed some $30 million in venture funding, and in 1982 he, Hannah, and a small group of other doctoral students founded SGI.

In 1984 the company provided filmmaker George Lucas, the creator of the Star Wars movies, with a prototype of a high-powered computer workstation Hannah had helped innovate. Thanks to Lucas's influence, SGI quickly became well known in the film industry, and graphics software Hannah developed was used to create effects for such hit movies as *Jurassic Park*, *Terminator 2*, *Aladdin*, *Beauty and the Beast*, and *Field of Dreams*, among others. (In 1995 the first feature-length animated movie to be entirely generated by computer, *Toy Story*, was created with SGI's workstations.)

Directors were thrilled that the animation process no longer had to be done painstakingly by hand, frame by frame, and use of SGI products quickly spread to other industries; for example, SGI technology has been used by biomedical firms to sequence genes and by the military in visual simulators, among other applications. The company once partnered with Nintendo to help create the Nintendo 64 gaming system, "effectively cramming the power of a $5,000 SGI Indy workstation into a $250 toy," as one journalist observed.

In 1986—the year the company went public—Hannah was named its principal scientist, and two years later, in 1988, he won a prestigious Black Engineer of the Year Award for technical achievement. In 1997 he left SGI to become the vice president of media production and technology at Omniverse Digi-

Hannah and SGI played a part in the Terminator movies, among many others.

tal Solutions, a Virginia-based startup, and in later years he accepted a post at Pulsent, a company involved with **video compression**. (He also helped a friend develop a short-lived venture called SongPro, which manufactured a plug-in music cartridge for the Nintendo system.)

While not in the public eye in recent years, Hannah will long be remembered as the innovator who helped George Lucas, Steven Spielberg, and other moviemakers bring their creative visions to the big screen. ●

Words to Understand

manufacturing engineer
an engineer whose job involves the research, design, and development of industrial systems, processes, machines, and equipment

SMS
an acronym for Short Message Service, the transmission of text messages of no more than 160 alpha-numeric characters (with no images or graphics) to and from a mobile phone, fax machine, or IP address

Chapter 5

Herman Chinery-Hesse

Born:
1965

Nationality:
Ghanaian

Achievements:
Technology entrepreneur and promoter of programming and services in Africa

In the early 1990s, the sub-Saharan African nation of Ghana seemed like an unlikely place to start a technology company. The country had been ruled by oppressive military governments for decades, and even after a constitutional democracy was instituted in 1992 and Ghana's economy began to stabilize, founding any business remained a daunting process, thanks to hard-to-navigate business regulations and little institutional support for entrepreneurs.

Now, however, Ghana boasts a thriving entrepreneurial culture and numerous tech companies, and much of the change is due to Herman Chinery-Hesse, who is often called the Bill Gates of Africa. Chinery-Hesse is the founder of SOFTtribe, the first and largest software company in the country; many of his employees have gone on to start firms of

their own, transforming Ghana into one of the most important hubs of technology on the African continent.

A large man with a booming laugh, he jokes that while his nickname is flattering and could motivate young people to emulate him, "I certainly don't have the kind of wealth that Bill Gates has."

Chinery-Hesse was born in 1965 in Dublin, Ireland, when his Ghanaian-born parents were studying at Trinity College for careers in international diplomacy. Because of the demands of their jobs, the family moved frequently, and Chinery-Hesse spent time in Zambia, Sierra Leone, Geneva, Uganda, and Tanzania, among other locales.

Back in Ghana for high school, he attended the prestigious Mfantsipim School, and upon graduating, he moved to the U.S., where he studied industrial technology at Texas State University. Chinery-Hesse felt ambivalent about America. While he was subject to racist taunts from some of his classmates, he appreciated the business opportunities and sense of possibility that he found.

Chinery-Hesse believed that business could be good back home in Ghana.

Upon earning his bachelor's degree in 1988, Chinery-Hesse moved to England, where he found work as a **manufacturing engineer**. On a Christmas visit to Ghana in 1990, however, he decided to remain there. His friends were skeptical—many of them were trying to find jobs outside the country—but Chinery-Hesse was determined. He told one interviewer, "[In America or Europe] it would be an uphill battle, whereas in Ghana the sky was the limit. Also I'm African: we need development here and it's Africans who are going to develop Africa. I felt a sense of responsibility, apart from the fact that I thought I'd have a brighter future here."

Initially, he considered entering the manufacturing sector, but he lacked the money to set up a factory. His personal computer, he realized, was "a factory that required no capital, only brainpower," as he once told a journalist. He soon found a job with the largest travel agency in Ghana, which hired him to write a software program that automated its accounting and customer service tasks. The program was so effective that it was adopted by travel agents throughout the country and became the industry standard.

Next, Chinery-Hesse, working on an old computer in his bedroom, modified that program so that it could be used by any business to track sales. With the help of a former classmate, Chinery-Hesse began installing his new program and providing technical support for a growing roster of clients. (The first major contract ever awarded to SOFTtribe, as he named his enterprise, was for a $5,000 job to computerize a large chicken farm.)

In quick succession, Chinery-Hesse developed an inventory-management system that became popular with grocery stores, a payroll system that is now ubiquitous throughout Ghana, a text-messaging application, and a system used by managers of Internet cafés. By 2003, SOFTtribe had grown from two old friends sharing a single computer in Chinery-Hesse's childhood bedroom to a team of eighty. (Chinery-Hesse had finally been forced to find real office space when his parents returned from a trip abroad only to find their home overrun with software engineers and computers crammed into any free spot.)

In addition to homegrown Ghanaian companies, large multinationals doing business in Africa began employing Chinery-Hesse's software. His clients eventually included such major players as Unilever, Nestlé, and Guinness. He has recalled that when he won the Nestlé contract, he was still using rudimentary, makeshift office space, and executives for the company appeared horrified when they visited. Luckily, Chinery-Hesse had almost completed their project, winning them over with his technical savvy and programming competence despite the less-than-luxurious surroundings.

In late 2004 SOFTtribe became a Microsoft partner, selling and installing the American software giant's products in Ghana and rewriting Chinery-Hesse's applications to work within Microsoft's offerings. Even Ghana's president praised the move as a step forward for the African tech industry, and SOFTtribe began winning government contracts to modernize the national ID card program and federal payroll system, among other assignments.

Not content to rest on his laurels (and reportedly slightly disgruntled at being compelled to deal with Microsoft), in 2007 Chinery-Hesse launched a second company, Black Star Line (BSL), which he described as "the eBay of Africa, but also an African PayPal in that it harnesses the power of the Internet and **SMS** to enable global trade with this continent."

Chinery-Hesse fervently believes that technology is not only improving the lives of his countrymen but changing the entrepreneurial landscape of Ghana for the better. "The ubiquity of new platforms and the potential technological product development possibilities thereof definitely represent a game-changing moment in African history," he has written. "For techies like myself, we have appreciated the virgin African environment with its peculiar challenges that nevertheless have helped to unleash our creative juices. We have been called upon to bring innovative solutions to problems right to the doorstep of the disadvantaged as well as those in the remotest parts of our continent, linking us to an increasingly globalized world." ●

Chinery-Hesse often mentors young people looking at science careers.

Words to Understand

dismay
shock and surprise

plummeted
fell rapidly from a great distance

Chapter 6

Kimberly Bryant

Born:
1967

Nationality:
American

Achievements:
Computer scientist
and nonprofit founder of
Black Girls Code

"The glory of being the first black female Mark Zuckerberg is up for grabs, and Kimberly Bryant is making sure that there will be enough girls to step lively over the digital divide," a journalist wrote for the online publication *The Root*, which deemed Bryant one of the 100 most important African Americans of 2013. Bryant is the founder of the nonprofit group Black Girls Code, which seeks to introduce programming and technology to a new generation of coders, who will, she predicts "become builders of technological innovation and of their own futures."

Kimberly Bryant was born on January 14, 1967, and was raised in Memphis, Tennessee. She studied several instruments but most enjoyed playing the bass drum in her elementary-school marching band. She has described herself as a "nerdy girl," who eagerly joined

her high-school math team and took honors courses in science, despite there being few role models in her inner-city neighborhood. (Neither of her parents had a background in science or math.) After graduating from Memphis Central High, she entered Vanderbilt University. At the advice of a guidance counselor who knew she excelled at science and math, she majored in electrical engineering.

Bryant was excited to take a course in computer programming as a college freshman, and she loved mastering Fortran and Pascal, then the most popular languages for novice programmers. While she enjoyed her classes and had many friends, she has recalled feeling somewhat isolated. "Few of my classmates looked like me," she once wrote. "While we shared similar aspirations and many good times, there's much to be said for making any challenging journey with people of the same cultural background."

Bryant graduated with her bachelor's degree in 1989 and immediately embarked upon her career, working for a year as an engineer at the Westinghouse

```
62  <!--<h3 id="fotovirs"><? if ($_COOKIE['lang'] =='eng'){
63       echo "Photo gallery";}
64       elseif ($_COOKIE['lang'] =='rus') {
65       echo "Фотогалерея";
66  }
67  else
68       echo "Foto galerija";
69       ?></h3>-->
70
71  <div class="<?if($_GET[type]==1|||$_GET[type]}echo"current";?>">
72      <a href="foto-galerija.php?type=1@text_margin">
73          <div id="left_sidebar">
74              <div id="left_ico"> </div>
75              <p <?if($_COOKIE['lang'] =='rus')echo "style="margin:0px"">
76  <?
77  if($_COOKIE['lang'] =='eng'){
78       echo "Wood-frame houses";
79  }elseif($_COOKIE['lang'] =='rus'){
80       echo "Деревянные каркасные дома";
81  }else{
82       echo "Koka karkasa mājas";
```

Computer programmers use words and symbols to describe a series of actions to a computer.

Electric Company before moving on to become a supervisor at DuPont, a chemical firm. In 1995 she began supervising almost 100 mechanical and electrical workers at Phillip Morris International, overseeing an annual budget of more than $5 million. She subsequently took posts at the pharmaceutical giants Merck, Pfizer, and Novartis, as well as at the biotechnology firm Genentech.

After more than two decades at large companies, Bryant, then living in the San Francisco Bay Area, decided to explore the world of startups. She was dismayed to discover that it was a world largely made up of Caucasian men. Her **dismay** only increased when she sent her 10-year-old daughter to a computer science camp being held for middle-school students at Stanford. Avidly interested in learning how to create computer games, Bryant's daughter was one of the few girls in the group and the only person (boy or girl) of color. She explained to her mother that the instructors at the camp seemed to be focused more intently on the boys, ignoring questions from the girls and giving them scant guidance during hands-on activities.

Bryant was appalled. "That's when the issues came together personally and professionally," she told one interviewer. "I didn't want her to be unmotivated and feel like she couldn't learn these skills or thrive because of the attention she got in class."

After Bryant attended a Berkeley conference for female entrepreneurs a few months later, she was moved to action. Panelists at the conference had been complaining about the

lack of qualified women who could be hired to fill tech jobs, blaming the industry's lack of diversity on the fact that few women—of any ethnicity—were interested in science, technology, engineering, and math (STEM). "When you do a survey of girls in middle school, more than half express an interest in STEM careers in the future, but by the time they get to high school, that number has plummeted down to single digits," Bryant lamented to one interviewer. "Now, when we look at girls of color and communities of color, there is an additional challenge that we're facing with students from underrepresented communities not even getting early access to STEM careers and opportunities. The role models and the potential career paths they see don't typically include jobs in tech or going to work for Google or Facebook."

In 2011, soon after that conference, Bryant launched Black Girls Code, with the mission of changing the situation. She initially mounted workshops for just 20 or so girls at a time, right in the San Francisco Bay Area, but in 2012 she launched the Summer of Code project, intending to reach girls in seven different cities over the course of three months. By the end of the summer, some 80 girls at a time were squeezing into classes in Atlanta, Detroit, Chicago, and New York, among other places. Black Girls Code now has numerous official chapters across the United States, and one in Johannesburg, South Africa, with classes being led by volunteer mentors from such major companies as Microsoft and Google.

Because there are always job vacancies for programmers, the group's focus was initially on coding, but it has expanded in recent years to other STEM topics; among the most popular offerings are those involving robotics or gaming. Bryant has announced an ambitious goal of reaching one million

The goal of groups like Bryant's is to expose people to programming at a young age.

girls by 2040. (She has also announced the impending formation of a "brother" organization, Black Boys Code.)

Bryant—who was named one of the 25 Most Influential African Americans in Technology by the editors of *Business Insider* magazine, and the recipient of a 2014 Smithsonian Ingenuity Award—tirelessly travels to promote her cause and raise funds to expand the organization. "We are hoping to teach our girls to be builders and not just consumers. We need to teach them to solve problems, hack the issues that are important to them," she says. "We must be sure that girls have a seat at the table. If we empower them and uplift them then we will create solutions that will create a better world for us all." ●

Kimberly Bryant:
Inspiration leader in tech

Words to Understand

peripatetic
moving or traveling from place to place

Clarence Wooten

Born:
1971

Nationality:
American

Achievements:
Web design entrepreneur and technology investor

omeone who has a great business idea and ends up starting a company is called an entrepreneur, but what about when a person is bursting with several great ideas? If they go on to launch business after business, it's now common to refer to them as serial entrepreneurs, and thanks to the ubiquity and affordability of computing devices, many of them can be found in the tech industry.

Look no further than Clarence Wooten as a prime example. From starting his first company as a college freshman, to selling another of his early startups in 1999 for $23 million, to presiding over two promising new ventures as this is being written (and, in all likelihood, others in the near future), Wooten is helping redefine what it means to be a businessperson in the 21st century.

Wooten was born in Baltimore, Mary-

land, in 1971. His father, Clarence Sr., initially worked in the steel mills, while his mother, Cecilia, was a seamstress. Neither had attended college, but both harbored a strong desire to be more independent and less beholden to employers. Clarence Sr. began buying properties to rent, and Cecilia opened a small assisted living facility, which she ran with the help of her sisters.

Despite their solid work ethic, finances were sometimes rocky, and the family moved within the Baltimore area numerous times—living in a pleasant suburb when they could afford to and returning to the inner city when times were hard. That **peripatetic** lifestyle meant that Wooten was forced to transfer in and out of school systems; by the time he had graduated from 12th grade, he had attended eight different schools. Realizing that his parents' budgetary difficulties were largely the result of not attending college, he vowed that he would get a good education, and he dreamed of becoming a millionaire one day. (He has admitted that the popular television shows of the era, like *Fantasy Island* and *Dynasty*, which depicted the lifestyles of the ultra-wealthy, played some part in fueling that dream.)

Like many teens, Wooten was an avid fan of video games, but he rarely had money to buy all the titles he wanted to play. Using a Commodore 64 home computer equipped with a modem, however, he and his friends were able to "crack" the copyright protection of any game within days of its official release. They would then add their own intro screen to the game and distribute their version to a select group of others in the gaming underworld who also had recently pirated games to share.

Wooten explained, "I eventually ran my own bulletin board, Kastle Kaoz....Our group was the biggest in the world on the Commodore 64 for 6-7 months.

Wooten went from using this early computer called a Commodore 64 to become a tech leader.

So it was like being an entrepreneur, like being part of the Fortune 500, when you think of it." He makes plain, however, that he and his friends had no intention of selling the games for profit. "It was more of a Robin Hood thing," he says. "We made the games we cracked available only to a few other kids like us. We weren't motivated by money but by the chance to show off our skills. I got to interact with kids like me from all over the world at the age of 13, and I always thought of our activities in terms of 'liberating' the games or making them open-source." Looking back as an adult, Wooten is exceedingly grateful not to have been apprehended for his activities, and he stresses that no aspiring young tech entrepreneur should emulate him in that respect.

Thinking that he might want to pursue architecture as a profession, Wooten—a skilled basketball player who had been a valued member of his high school team and who continued to play as an undergraduate—initially earned an associate's degree in computer-aided design (CAD) for Architecture and Engineering from Maryland's Catonsville Community College. There, one of his computer programs

won a competition held by *CADalyst* magazine. In 1991, while he was still an undergraduate, Wooten founded his first company, Envision Designs, which transformed an architect's drawings into 3D computer-generated walk-through animations. That experience led to a summer consulting job, launching an in-house CAD division for an established architectural firm.

With Andre Forde, a slightly older grad with similar interests, the two launched a firm, Metamorphosis Studios, which developed presentations and interactive brochures for clients.

The pair subsequently founded ImageCafé, which provided a wide variety of templates so that small businesses could build their own high-quality websites. They reasoned, correctly, that most small companies could not afford high-end design services, which typically charged several thousand dollars to build a site; nor did most businessmen want to take the time to learn the do-it-yourself software that would enable them to create a rudimentary site on their own. Using a ready-made customizable "master" from ImageCafé allowed a business to save money while still getting a professional-looking end product.

Within a year of launching the new venture, Wooten, who had earned a B.S. in Business Management from Johns Hopkins University by then, sold ImageCafé to a large company called Network Solutions for $23 million.

Although he might have easily retired while still in his 20s to enjoy his newfound wealth, Wooten has since founded several other enterprises. Among the most recent of these is Groupsite.com, an online platform that combines social networking and collaborative tools. Wooten has also launched an enterprise called Progressly.com, which aims to improve the business practices of its clients by enabling them to monitor, improve, and replicate their work processes (for example, negotiating a lease or hiring a new employee) by using cloud-based visual charts.

Wooten has also been involved in providing capital to promising new ventures and feels strongly about helping minority entrepreneurs—who often have a hard time attracting seed money—to get their start. To that end, he recently launched VentureFund.io, which allows young businesses to showcase their success and growth metrics online, and in turn, allows investors to make purely data-driven decisions about which ventures to back.

Once a young entrepreneur has won backing and launched a successful business, Wooten says suitors will almost certainly emerge. His advice if that happens: sell the company to the highest bidder with the best structured offer for you and your investors, take a long vacation, put money away for safe keeping, and then, "Start another company, because it's in your blood." ●

Clarence Wooten:
Investor and entrepreneur

Words to Understand

hackathon
an event in which a large number of people meet to intensively engage in collaborative computer programming

propensity
an inclination or tendency to behave in a certain way

IT
an acronym for Information Technology, a field that encompasses the tools, processes, and equipment employed to collect, process, and present information. In broader terms, IT also includes office automation and telecommunications.

Hadiyah Mujhid

Born:
1979

Nationality:
American

Achievements:
**Technology entrepreneur
and engineer who created
an incubator to help
other companies**

I n addition to co-founding her own software-development company, Playpen Labs, Hadiyah Mujhid is one of the organizers of the nonprofit group Black Founders, which is dedicated to increasing the number of successful black entrepreneurs in technology through networking meetings, educational programs, **hackathons**, and other such events.

Mujhid was born in 1979 in Philadelphia, Pennsylvania. Her mother had emigrated from Jamaica, seeking expanded educational opportunities and a better way of life. Determined to become a registered nurse, she regularly worked during the day and took classes at night, all while raising Mujhid and her two younger sisters.

Mujhid's stepfather was a bus driver who worked a full day and then often signed

on for evening charter trips to earn extra money. When Mujhid's mother had to be at a class, the three girls, then too young to be left home by themselves, would accompany their stepfather on the bus, riding from Philadelphia to Atlantic City and back again over the space of a long evening. Mujhid cites her parents' work ethic and tenacity—enrolling for a class or two at a time, it took her mother a decade to earn her R.N. degree—as major sources of inspiration.

Working that hard to provide for the family, neither parent was too pleased when Mujhid showed a **propensity** for taking electronics apart—particularly when she could not put them back together again, as happened with a VCR player on one memorable occasion.

Naturally gifted in math and science, Mujhid found that she could essentially coast in her classes at Masterman High, a competitive public school in Philadelphia. That ethos did not serve her well once she had graduated in 1997 and entered the pre-med program at the University of Maryland Eastern Shore, a historically black institution in the town of Princess Anne. With organic chemistry giving her particular trouble, she began trying to think of a different path—one that would not upset her parents, who had hoped that she might enter a prestigious, well-paying profession like medicine or law.

Mujhid had worked during the summers for an uncle who ran an **IT** business, and there she had learned basic HTML (Hypertext Markup Language) and CSS (Cascading Style Sheets), both essential for building Web pages. Still un-

Mujhid put her engineering skills to work helping to build Navy warships.

sure of an exact career path but remembering that she had enjoyed learning those technologies, she switched her major to computer science during her sophomore year.

Mujhid earned her B.S. in 2001, and even before she had graduated, she had lined up a job as a software engineer at Lockheed Martin, a major security and aerospace company that produces advanced technology systems, products, and services. One of her proudest moments, she has recalled, was showing her parents the formal job-offer letter, which mentioned a salary larger than any either of them had ever made.

Mujhid began work in June 2001 and was assigned to develop software applications for Navy ships. When the terrorist attacks of 9/11 occurred, just months after she was hired, she was assigned to projects relating to domestic security and has expressed pride that her work may have helped saved lives. She ultimately remained at Lockheed Martin for almost a dozen years.

During her last few years with the company, Mujhid had watched with interest as mobile computing and consumer software came to the fore. When she was transferred to a

Lockheed Martin office in the San Francisco Bay Area—a hub of startup culture—she became even more intrigued. Despite her parents' disbelief that she would quit a stable, lucrative job, Mujhid decided to make the leap into independent software development. The next few years were a time of personal growth and learning by doing.

On a personal level, her mother had recently been diagnosed with pancreatic cancer, and leaving Lockheed Martin allowed Mujhid the freedom to move back home and care for her. Spending the final year of her mother's life by her side was, Mujhid has explained, an irreplaceable experience for which she'll always be grateful. On a professional level, Mujhid began to discover just what it took to launch a startup. She worked to build a photo-sharing app called Picture.ly, joined a consulting firm called Thunderbolt Labs, and along with three friends and fellow entrepreneurs (Chris Bennett, Nnena Ukuku, and Monique Woodard) launched the nonprofit organization Black Founders.

While she expected Black Founders' first meeting to attract only ten people or so, twice that many showed up, and the group has since expanded greatly. It now hosts regular networking events and conferences in cities across the country, and among its flagship projects is HBCUHacks, weekend-long hackathons that give students at historically black colleges and universities the opportunity to practice coding and work together to build mobile apps and Web software.

In 2013 Mujhid and her husband, Morten Lundsby Jensen, formerly of Google, launched Playpen Labs. The two describe the enterprise as a "tech startup on our own terms" and develop only projects for which they feel a deep affinity. HBCURecruit, to give just one example, is a platform that allows companies to attract students and alumni of more than 100 historically black colleges and universities with a single click. (Playpen also works with outside clients on help-desk consulting, Web development, user research and testing, and other such areas.)

Mujhid holds an MBA from Drexel University and teaches at the San Francisco-based Hackbright Academy, a software engineering school for women. She once wrote, "I am a black female developer entrepreneur. I am diversity in tech. I don't need to talk about it anymore than it's already been talked about. I don't need to go write about it anymore than it's been written about. I need to 'be about it.' And that's what I and a large community of others are doing. Being about it." ●

Hadiyah Mujhid:
Engineer turned incubator

Careers in Technology

ccording to recent studies by the National Black Information Technology Leadership Organization (NBITLO) and the US Bureau of Labor Statistics, blacks hold well under 10 percent of all information technology jobs in the U.S.—and fewer than 3 percent of the leadership positions in those fields.

Some experts attribute this to a phenomenon called the "digital divide," the growing gap between the economically and educationally disadvantaged members of society who lack access to computers and those who take such access for granted. Others assert that universities aren't doing a good job recruiting a broad mix of students for technology degrees or that black students are not even interested in those fields.

No matter what the reason, it's vitally important to change that situation, because

diversity is crucial to technological innovation. Diverse groups of people see problems differently and can team up to solve them faster and better! (Who knows how long it would have taken Fairchild to manufacture the interchangeable game cartridge without Jerry Lawson!)

Whether you want to program the next best-selling video game, develop your own app, or start your own tech company, it's important to take as many high-level math and science courses as possible. But you can start even before high school. Many universities and other organizations (like Black Girls Code) offer afterschool or summer

For many fans of technology, getting their hands on the insides of the machines is a great way to start.

programs that can provide basic instruction and practical, hands-on experience to help determine whether a high-tech career is right for you.

Just Google "technology programs for teens," and a wealth of possibilities shows up—from Tech Kids Unlimited, which provides a wide range of interesting courses for students with learning disabilities, to the National Youth Science Camp, which runs challenging programs for youths from across the country and around the world.

One point on which everyone agrees: despite any lingering stereotypes, technologists do not have to be white or Asian men. They do not have to fit any mold. The popular image of the skinny, eyeglass-wearing, Vitamin D-deficient geek sporting a company hoodie is totally outmoded. Technologists have, in reality, always come in all colors, genders, and sizes—and from all different backgrounds. And anyone who has the skills and talent can and should find a place in the tech world. ●

Text-Dependent Questions

1. What was the Illiac IV?

2. In what year was the Fairchild Channel F game console introduced?

3. What instruments did John W. Thompson play as a young man?

4. How much venture capital did it take to launch SGI?

5. What was the first major contract ever awarded to SOFT-tribe?

6. What were the most popular computer languages for novice programmers back in the 1980s?

7. What is a serial entrepreneur?

8. Which family member first introduced Hadiyah Mujhid to working with computers?

Suggested Research Projects

1. Home video games have come a long way since Pong entranced users. In addition to Jerry Lawson's interchangeable game cartridges, what are some of the technical innovations that have led to the sophisticated games now on the market?

2. *Toy Story* was the first animated feature film to be entirely generated by computer. Research which other films were subsequently created this way. How are they different from traditional animated films?

3. Herman Chinery-Hesse helped start a wave of high-tech companies in Ghana. Try to find out which other companies have launched since he founded SOFTtribe. Which have been started by his former employees?

4. Look up the group Black Girls Code. Find out if it offers classes or workshops near you. If not, write a letter to Kimberly Bryant explaining why there is a need for the program in your neighborhood.

5. Serial entrepreneurs must be adventurous and willing to take risks. Make a list of some of the other traits business experts say they must also display.

Find Out More

Websites

www.code.org
is a website with great games and activities devoted to helping students learn the fundamentals of coding and computer science. It is run by an organization dedicated to the idea that STEM learning is for everyone.

www.tynker.com
allows students to develop games and apps, interface with computer hardware, and more.

www.takeitgoanywhere.org
explores the field of Information Technology (IT), related careers, and the education needed to pursue them.

Books

McManus, Sean. *How to Code in 10 Easy Lessons: Learn How to Design and Code Your Very Own Computer Game*. Irvine, CA: Walter Foster Publishing, 2015.

Sande, Warren and Carter Sande. *Hello World!: Computer Programming for Kids and Other Beginners*. Shelter Island, NY: Manning Publications, 2013.

McDowell, Gayle Laakmann. *Cracking the Tech Career*. Hoboken, NJ: Wiley, 2014.

Series Glossary of Key Terms

botany the study of plant biology

electron a negatively charged particle in an atom

genome all the DNA in an organism, including all the genes

nanometer a measurement of length that is one-billionth of a meter

nanotechnology manipulation of matter on an atomic or molecular scale

patent a set of exclusive rights granted to an inventor for a limited period of time in exchange for detailed public disclosure of an invention

periodic table the arrangement of all the known elements into a table based on increasing atomic number

protein large molecules in the body responsible for the structure and function of all the tissues in an organism

quantum mechanics the scientific principles that describe how matter on a small scale (such as atoms and electrons) behaves

segregated separated, in this case by race

ultraviolet a type of light, usually invisible, that can cause damage to the skin

Index

Photo credits

About the Author

Mari Rich was educated at Lehman College, part of the public City University of New York. As a writer and editor, she has had many years of experience in the fields of university communications and reference publishing, most notably with the highly regarded periodical *Current Biography*, aimed at high school and college readers. She also edited and wrote for *World Authors, Leaders of the Information Age,* and *Nobel Laureates.* Currently, she spends much of her time writing about engineers and engineering.